KU-283-081

BRUCE LEE

BRUCE LEE

WORDS FROM A MASTER

EDITED BY JOHN R. LITTLE
FOREWORD BY ROBERT WOLFF

CB
CONTEMPORARY BOOKS

Library of Congress Cataloging-in-Publication Data

Lee Bruce, 1940–1973.

    Bruce Lee : words from a master / edited by John R. Little ;
foreword by Robert Wolff.
      p.   cm.
    ISBN 0-8092-2856-4
    1. Lee, Bruce, 1940–1973—Interviews.   2. Actors—United
States—Interviews.   3. Martial artists—United States—Interviews.
I. Little, John R., 1960– .   II. Title.
PN2287.L2897A5   1998
791.43′028′092—dc21   98-6795
                                          CIP

Cover design by Todd Petersen
Interior design by Amy Yu Ng

Published by Contemporary Books
A division of NTC/Contemporary Publishing Group, Inc.
4255 West Touhy Avenue, Lincolnwood (Chicago), Illinois 60646-1975 U.S.A.
Copyright © 1999 by John R. Little and Robert Wolff
All rights reserved. No part of this book may be reproduced, stored in a
retrieval system, or transmitted in any form or by any means, electronic,
mechanical, photocopying, recording, or otherwise, without the prior
permission of NTC/Contemporary Publishing Company.
Manufactured in the United States of America
International Standard Book Number: 0-8092-2856-4
98 99 00 01 02 03 BG 17 16 15 14 13 12 11 10 9 8 7 6 5 4 3 2 1

Words from a Master

Empty your mind. Be formless, shapeless—like water. If you put water into a cup, it becomes the cup. You put water into a bottle, it becomes the bottle. You put it in a teapot, it becomes the teapot. Now, water can flow or it can crash. Be water, my friend.

When I first learned martial art, I too challenged many established instructors and, of course, some others challenged me. But I have learned that challenging means one thing to you: What is your reaction to it? How does it get you? If you are secure within yourself, you treat it very lightly because you ask yourself, Am I really afraid of that man? Do I have any doubts or fear that he might get me? And if I do not have such doubts and such fears, then I would certainly treat it very lightly, just as if today the rain is coming down very strong but tomorrow, baby, the sun is going to come out again.

Man is always in a learning process, whereas a [martial arts] "style" is a concluded, established, solidified something. You cannot do that, because you learn every day as you grow older.

The original founder of [each martial arts] style started out with hypothesis. But now it has become the gospel truth, and people who go into that become the product of it. It doesn't matter how you are, who you are, how you are structured, how you are built or how you are made . . . it doesn't seem to matter. You just go in there and *be* that product. And that, to me, is not right.

If [a martial art] is a sport, then you are now talking about something else; you have regulations, you have rules. But if you are talking about fighting—as it is; that is to say, with no rules—well, then, baby, you had better train every part of your body!

All types of knowledge . . . ultimately means self-knowledge.

In the beginning, I had no intention whatsoever that what I was practicing, and what I'm still practicing now, would lead to this.

[Success] hasn't changed me, basically because I know that in my [life], something simply happened which is breaking some records. It doesn't mean anything, you know. It's just something that *happened*. It didn't give me any reason to think that I should be proud or that I'm any better than I ever was.

When you become successful, when you become famous, it's very, very easy to be blinded by all these happenings. Everybody comes up to you and it's "Mister Lee." When you have long hair, they'll say, "Hey, man, that's 'in'; that's the 'in' thing." But if you have no name, they will say, "Boy, look at the disgusting juvenile delinquent!" Unless you realize what life is all about, and that right now some game is happening—and realize that it is a game—fine and dandy. That's all right. But most people tend to be blinded by it, because if things are repeated too many times, you believe them. And that can become a habit.

Whenever I look around I always learn one thing, and that is: always be yourself, . . . express yourself, have faith in yourself. Do not go out and look for a successful personality and duplicate him.

To me, ultimately, martial art means honestly expressing your-self. Now it is very difficult to do. It is easy for me to put on a show and be cocky and then feel pretty cool. Or I can do all kinds of phony things. Or I can show you some really fancy movement. But to express oneself honestly, not lying to one-self—that, my friend, is very hard to do.

Nowadays you don't go around on the street kicking people or punching people, because if you do [someone will simply pull out a gun and]—BANG! That's it. I mean, I don't care how good you are.

I have no fear of an opponent in front of me. I'm very self-sufficient, and they do not bother me. And, should I fight— should I do anything—I have made up my mind that, baby, you had better kill me before I get you.

If I tell you I'm good, probably you will say that I'm boasting. But if I tell you I'm not good, you'll know I'm lying.

Commentaries on Bruce Lee

It seems we were always beginning on a new life—beginning in films was a new life for us. Becoming famous and breaking records—everything was new all the time, and he kept saying, "This is just the beginning." He had a long way to go, so many more things he wanted to do. And he also thought of it as a beginning for the Chinese people, what they have to show to the rest of the world. He was very proud of being Chinese, and he wanted to show the rest of the world part of the Chinese culture through films.

Linda Lee Cadwell
Bruce Lee's widow

When I first met Bruce, I could not handle being around him very long. He was an unending bundle of energy and a typical teenager. Very shortly thereafter, however, I was captivated by the depth of this young man's character. He could be telling a raunchy joke one minute, and then hold forth on the philosophy of Taoism and Zen the next. There was also a warmth of "charisma" that flowed from him; when Bruce walked into your presence, you were somehow mesmerized by that magnetic personality and that unique laugh. And when these were complemented with that sincere, almost childlike, smile of his, you couldn't help but like him. It is not often that such a young man can come into one's life and teach a secret that cannot be measured in terms of dollars—self-identity. To this day, there sparkle in my mind jewels of thought that he knew someday in the future I would understand.

Taky Kimura
Bruce Lee's closest friend and
senior student

He was an idol for so many. The great thing about someone like Bruce Lee is that he inspires so many millions and millions of kids out there who want to follow in his footsteps. They want to become martial artists; they want to be in movies. And so, what they do is go out and train every day for hours and hours. Bruce Lee provided tremendous inspiration; he served to help so many kids around the world. He had a profound and tremendous impact worldwide, and I think he will be admired for a long time. He was one of a kind.

Arnold Schwarzenegger
from an interview published in
Bruce Lee *magazine*

I learned a lot from him. He was a very knowledgeable individual; his whole life was the martial arts. . . . They'll never find somebody as good.

Chuck Norris
from an interview published in
Hands of Kung Fu *magazine*

Bruce Lee was a great man. He was truly one of a kind. I wish now that I could have met him because I really liked his style. He was way ahead of his time.

Muhammad Ali

Contents

FOREWORD BY ROBERT WOLFF   XV

PREFACE   XVII

PART I: BRUCE LEE IN CONVERSATION WITH
          PIERRE BERTON   1

In this interview with Canadian journalist and author Pierre Berton, Lee reveals his philosophy of combat, the difference between tournament karate and street fighting, the Hong Kong movie industry, his philosophy of life, and how he wished to be remembered.

PART II: PIERRE BERTON REFLECTS ON INTERVIEWING
           BRUCE LEE   21

Pierre Berton, the man who conducted what is considered to be the most in-depth interview ever recorded with Lee, offers insight into the origins of the interview, its impact, and the significance of Lee in this fascinating appreciation of one man's incredible legacy.

PART III: BRUCE LEE IN CONVERSATION WITH
            TED THOMAS   33

Lee is at his most engaging as he answers questions posed to him by British broadcaster Ted Thomas during a 1971 Radio Hong Kong interview. Lee discusses such diverse topics as his friendship with celebrity students Steve McQueen and James Coburn, his appearance in *The Green Hornet*, his

unique approach to combat, and many other direct
questions regarding his life and career.

PART IV: TED THOMAS REFLECTS ON INTERVIEWING
        BRUCE LEE   45
Ted Thomas reflects on the experience of interviewing Lee,
and what it was to know Lee during the peak of his Hong
Kong superstardom. In addition, Thomas offers insight into
Lee's relationship with the Hong Kong press, and the
significance of Lee to the twentieth century.

PART V: BRUCE LEE IN CONVERSATION WITH
        ALEX BEN BLOCK   59
While researching an article on martial arts for *Esquire*
magazine, New York journalist Alex Ben Block interviews
Lee via telephone while Lee is in Hong Kong filming *The
Way of the Dragon*. Lee speaks in great detail about his life,
his success, how he was adjusting to superstardom, and the
philosophical foundation of *jeet kune do*.

PART VI: ALEX BEN BLOCK REFLECTS ON INTERVIEWING
         BRUCE LEE   77
Alex Ben Block recollects his fascinating interview with
Lee and the history of the interview itself, offering insight
into the unparalleled scope and significance of Lee's films
and philosophy.

Foreword

Life can be a curious thing. Why is it, for instance, that the majority of people are content with living to a ripe old age with their best music still within them? And then there are those rare others who put every ounce of passion, desire, commitment, focus, and relentless action into that which they love, with the result that they accomplish, experience, and become more in a few short years than all the others in a lifetime. Bruce Lee was one such person.

Bruce left us too soon, yet he left us a treasure of incalculable wealth—his words. It is through the power of his words—both written and recorded—that he can change your life. Growing up, I would hear the name Bruce Lee, but I never really understood or appreciated who this man was. It wasn't until years later that I reached that understanding, when my good friend John Little and I literally stumbled onto what is now regarded as the most significant video that Bruce Lee ever recorded—the "lost interview."

You see, in it was not the martial arts superstar the world came to love. No, in it was Bruce Lee, the man—the everyday, commonsense philosopher who could take the most complex subject and make it easy to understand. Yet, the lost interview was only the beginning.

Almost as if we were chosen for the task, extremely rare audio interviews with Bruce Lee by Alex Ben Block and Ted Thomas became available to us. Though our company was only beginning and on a shoestring budget, fate played its hand and allowed us to acquire the rights to these incredible audio recordings and video, all of which came with the unspoken promise to make Bruce's words and ideas known, not only to his legions of fans, but to all who hungered for them. In your hands are those words, spoken by a man of great conviction.

Bruce Lee's words hold the potential to change your life. No more will you be content to simply be a part of the majority. From Lee's words and example, you will learn that you are the shaper of your destiny, and that greatness, excellence, and success are all within your grasp. Generations not yet born will be influenced by the words and works of Bruce Lee, just as generations past have been. Dare I say, they will be influenced by yours too!

To your happiness and success.

Robert Wolff, Ph.D.

Preface

Bruce Lee continues to represent many different things to many different people. To countless minorities, he's the "chosen one," who proved that pride, determination, and self-belief can overcome all racial and social obstacles. To the poor, Lee represents a beacon of hope, providing positive reinforcement to their dreams of overcoming financial adversity and achieving a better life. To the frail and weak, Lee represents what can be achieved physically if you're willing to put forth the effort. To filmmakers and fans, he is a pioneer, having single-handedly created a new and exciting cinematic genre. To those of a philosophic bent, Lee embodies the philosophic method, recognizing no sacred cows and subjecting all beliefs to the solvent probe of reason. And, to martial artists everywhere, Bruce Lee is the one who broke the shackles of tradition, emancipating them to begin their own quest of personal fulfillment and enlightenment.

Unfortunately, like a vintage wine inadvertently served at a weekend party, Lee was gone before people realized what they had in their possession. Only a handful of individuals studied with Lee—and by the time word got out about his incredible talent and teachings, it was too late.

However, on three separate occasions, three different men from three different countries—Ted Thomas from England, Pierre Berton from Canada, and Alex Ben Block from the United States—had the foresight to track down this phenomenal human being and get him to agree to professionally produced (and in one case, videotaped) discussions. The result of their efforts and perspicacity have been documented within the pages of this book. Truly historically significant discussions, these dialogues have preserved for posterity the only surviving record of Bruce Lee the man (as opposed to Bruce Lee the actor), taking the time to speak with first-class journalists about his life, art, and career in unprecedented detail and candor.

To those who knew Lee personally, these interviews have captured the spirit of the man they loved so well: the vitality, the emotion, the passion, the vision. To those who never met Lee, these interviews are the closest thing to time travel, allowing us to go back to the early 1970s and see for ourselves what it was like to sit down, one-on-one, and talk with Bruce Lee.

And what dialogues they are! Lee is showcased at his charismatic best. Both his message and his passion are made crystal clear to the reader as Lee honestly expresses *himself*— the man behind the legend.

Decades have passed since Bruce Lee first captured the imagination of the world with his revolutionary teachings and vibrant personality. But the world he envisioned is still of the future. Greatness in human beings is often measured by the degree to which one chooses to fully embrace life and the decision to seek out one's own path. So, while these pages celebrate the legacy of the incomparable man known as Lee Siu Lung ("Lee Little Dragon"), the message that cries out is for you to be your own person and not be chained down to any style, method, or system that would restrict your view of the world.

In this era of ethnic strife and worldwide malaise, it's important to remember the great words of one who walked among us for a brief span of thirty-two years with a message of universality and brotherhood. He changed the world for Asian Americans, for martial artists everywhere, and for all seekers of truth who know the value of refusing to give up their dreams. In an odd way, he is still more alive than most of us, inspiring us to reach beyond our self-imposed limitations and realize our full and unique potential.

The book you are holding is not simply a tribute to a celebrity from a bygone era. It is, instead, a continuation of the adventure, an extension of the joy, a fulfillment of the promise, and a celebration of the life that was, and continues to be, Bruce Lee.

John Little

BRUCE LEE

Part I

Bruce Lee in Conversation with Pierre Berton

December 9, 1971
Hong Kong

Be formless, shapeless—like water.

The interview you are about to read is perhaps the most significant one ever granted by Bruce Lee. It will certainly raise the reader's awareness of Bruce Lee—the man, as opposed to the fighter or movie star. The text is taken from a transcript of Lee's only surviving television interview, in which he was given roughly twenty-five minutes to explain his life, career, and philosophy.

The words make it possible for those of us who never had the chance to meet the man called Bruce Lee to at least experience his aura, his intensity, and his teachings through this conversation. In this remarkable interview Lee waxes philosophical and talks in-depth about his life and career up until that point (it was recorded almost exactly two years prior to his filming the blockbuster *Enter the Dragon*, the film that made him an international star, and immediately after the runaway success of his first Chinese-language film, *The Big Boss*).

Pierre Berton, the Canadian journalist who conducted this historic interview, maintains that of all the people he has interviewed over his very illustrious career (which consists of more than two thousand individuals, including such heavyweights as Malcolm X and Jimmy Hoffa), none was as intense and riveting as Bruce Lee.

Bruce Lee faces a real dilemma. He's on the verge of stardom in the United States with a projected TV series on the horizon, but he's just achieved superstardom as a film actor here in Hong Kong. So, what does he choose, the East or the West? It's the kind of problem that most budding movie actors would welcome. He's the man who taught karate, judo, and Chinese boxing to James Garner, Steve McQueen, Lee Marvin, and James Coburn. The newest Mandarin superstar, known in the West for his performances in Batman, The Green Hornet, Ironside, *and* Longstreet. *His name is Bruce Lee—and he doesn't even speak Mandarin!*

How can you play in Mandarin movies if you don't even speak Mandarin? How do you do that?

Well, first of all, I speak only Cantonese, so there is quite a difference as far as pronunciation and things like that go.

So, somebody else's voice is used?

Definitely! Definitely!

You just make the words? Doesn't it sound strange when you go to the movies, especially in Hong Kong, in your own town, and you see yourself with someone else's voice?

Not really, because most of the Mandarin pictures done here [in Hong Kong] are dubbed anyway. I mean, in this regard, they shoot *without* sound. So, it doesn't make any difference.

Your lips never quite make the right words, do they?

Yeah, well that's where the difficulty lies, you see. The Cantonese have a different way of saying things—I mean different from the Mandarin. So, I have to find something similar to that in order to keep a kind of a feeling going behind that in my films—something matching the Mandarin deal. Does it sound complicated?

Just like in the silent picture days. I gather that in the movies made here the dialogue is pretty stilted anyway.

Yeah, I agree with you. To me, a motion picture is *motion*. You've got to keep the dialogue down to the *minimum*.

Did you look at many Mandarin movies before you started playing in your first one?

Yes.

What did you think of them?

Quality-wise, I would have to admit that it's not quite up to the standard [of the United States]. However, it is growing, and it is getting higher and higher and going toward that standard that I would term *quality*.

They say the secret of your success in The Big Boss, *the movie that rocketed you to stardom in Asia, was that you did your own fighting. As an expert in the various martial arts in China, what did you think of the fighting that you saw in the movies that you studied before you became a star?*

Definitely in the beginning, I had no intention whatsoever that what I was practicing, and what I'm still practicing now, would lead to this. But martial art has a very, very deep meaning as far as my life is concerned, because, as an actor, as a martial artist, as a human being, all these—I have learned from martial art.

Maybe for our audience who doesn't know, you might be able to explain what exactly you mean by martial art?

Martial art includes all the combative arts like karate, judo, Chinese *gung fu* or Chinese boxing, whatever you call it. All those. Like aikido, Korean karate—I could go on and on and on. It's a combative form of fighting. Some of them became sport, but some of them are still not. Some of them use, for instance, kicking to the groin, jabbing fingers into eyes, and things like that.

No wonder you're successful in it! The Chinese movies are full of this kind of action anyway—they needed a guy like you!

[laughs] *Violence*, man!

So, you didn't have to use a double when you moved into the motion picture role here?

No.

You did it all yourself?

Right.

Can you break five or six pieces of wood with your hand or your foot?

I'd probably break my hand and foot [laughs].

You set up a school in Hollywood, didn't you?

Yes.

For people like James Garner, Steve McQueen, and the others.

Yes.

Why would they want to learn Chinese martial art? Because of a movie role?

Not really. To me, at least the way that I teach it, all types of knowledge ultimately mean self-knowledge. So, these people are coming in and asking me to teach them, not so much how to defend themselves or how to do somebody in. Rather, they want to learn to express themselves through some movement, be it anger, be it determination or whatever. So, in other words, they're paying me to show them, in combative form, the *art of expressing the human body.*

Which is acting, in a sense, isn't it? Or it would at least be a useful tool for an actor to have.

It might sound too philosophical, but it's *unacting acting* or *acting unacting*.

You've lost me!

I have, huh? What I mean is that it is a *combination* of both. I mean [extends his left arm] here is natural instinct, and [extends his other arm] here is control [slowly brings his two fists together]. You are to combine the two in harmony. If you have one to the extreme [natural instinct], you'll be very unscientific, and if you have another to the extreme [control], you become all of a sudden *a mechanical man*, no longer a human being. So, it is a successful combination of both [again draws his two fists together]. Therefore, it is not pure *naturalness*, or pure *unnaturalness*. The ideal is *unnatural naturalness* or *natural unnaturalness*.

Yin/yang, eh?

Right [laughs]. Man, that's it.

One of your students, James Coburn, played in a movie called Our Man Flint, *in which he used karate. Was that what he learned from you?*

He started training with me *after* that film. You see, I do not actually teach karate, because I do not believe in *styles* anymore. I do not believe that there is such a thing as "the *Chinese* way of fighting" or "the *Japanese* way of fighting," or any other "way of fighting," because unless a human being has three arms and four legs, there can be no different form of fighting. Basically, we have only two hands and two feet. Styles tend to separate men, because they have their own doctrines, and [raises his fist like a fundamentalist preacher] then their doctrine becomes the gospel truth that you cannot change! But, if you do not have styles, if you just say, "Here I am as a human being: how can I express myself *totally* and *completely*?"—that way, you won't have a style, because style is a crystallization. This approach is a process of continuing growth.

You talk about "Chinese boxing." How does it differ from, say, Western boxing?

Well, first we use the feet.

Uh-huh, that's a start.

And then we use the elbow.

Do you use "the thumb" too?

You name it, man, we use it!

8

You use it all?

You have to, you see, because that is the expression of the human body. I mean *everything*—not just the hands! If it is a sport [such as Western boxing], then you are talking about something else. You have regulations; you have rules. But if you are talking about fighting—as it is, with no rules—well, then, baby, you had better train every part of your body! And when you do punch, you've got to put your whole hip into it and snap it, and get all your energy in there and make your fist into a real weapon.

I don't want to tangle with you in any dark alleys, I'll tell you that right now! What is the difference between Chinese boxing and what we see these old men doing at eight o'clock every morning on the rooftops and the parks called tai chi chuan or "shadow boxing"?

Well, actually, tai chi chuan is one school of Chinese boxing, too. I'm very glad to see these people up early every morning, because it shows that they are at least caring for their own bodies, right? That's a good sign. What you see them practicing is a slow form of exercise which is called tai chi chuan—you see, I'm speaking Mandarin just now [laughs]. In the Cantonese language it is referred to as *tai kik kune*. It's more of an exercise for the elderly, not so much for the young.

What is the reason behind it being performed in the slow-motion manner that I've seen?

Hand-wise, it's very slow, and the idea is to push the arms out, but at all times you are supposed to keep the continuity going. The movements involve different kinds of bending and stretching, with the idea that you are just to keep the motion going.

It looks very much like a form of ballet.

Yes, it is very much like that. To them the idea is "running water never grows stale," so you've got to just *keep on flowing*.

Of all your famous students—James Garner, Steve McQueen, Lee Marvin, James Coburn, Roman Polanski—who was the best? Who adapted best to the oriental form of exercise and defense that you teach?

That depends. As a fighter, Steve McQueen is pretty good in that department, because that son of a gun has got the toughness in him.

I see that in him on the screen.

Steve is the kind of a guy who will say, in a ready-to-fight sense, "All right, baby, here I am, man." And he's ready to do it! Now James Coburn, on the other hand, is a peace-loving man. I mean he's really, really nice.

Super mellow and all that! You know what I mean? He appreciates the philosophical part of martial art. Therefore, his understanding of it is deeper than Steve's. So, it's really hard to say. I mean it's different, depending on what *you're* looking for in martial art.

It's interesting that we in the West don't, and haven't since the days of the Greeks who did, combine philosophy and art with sport. But quite clearly the Asian attitude is that the three are facets of the same thing.

To me, ultimately, martial art means honestly expressing yourself. It is very difficult to do. It is easy for me to put on a show and be cocky and then feel pretty cool. Or I can do all kinds of phony things and be blinded by it. Or I can show you some really fancy movement. But to express oneself honestly, not lying to oneself—that, my friend, is very hard to do. You have to *train*, so that when you want it, it's there! When you want to move, you *are* moving. And when you move, you are determined to move. Not taking one inch, not anything less than that. If I want to punch, I'm going to do it! So, that is the type of thing you have to train yourself into with martial art; to become one with it. You think, and it *is* happening.

This is very un-Western, this attitude. We've been discussing mainly the Chinese martial arts, which include things like

Chinese boxing, karate, and judo, which is what you taught when you lived in Hollywood after you left the University of Washington, where you studied, of all things, philosophy! But perhaps a person can now understand why philosophy and martial arts go together. And one might assume that you got into films simply because you knew a lot of actors. However, I heard that you told someone that you got the job on The Green Hornet, *where you played Kato the chauffeur, because you were "the only Chinese-looking guy who could pronounce the name of the leading character—Britt Reid!"*

[Both laugh] I meant that as a joke, of course! And it's a heck of a name. Every time I said it I was superconscious! Really, that's another interesting thing. Let's say you learn to speak Chinese. It is not difficult to learn and speak the *words*. The hard thing, the difficult thing, is trying to figure out what is behind the meaning, or what brought on the expression and feelings behind those words. When I first arrived in the United States and I looked at a Caucasian, I often would not know whether he was putting me on or if he was really angry, because we have different ways of reacting. Those are the difficult things, you see?

Of course. It's almost as if you came upon a strange race where a smile doesn't mean what it does to us. In fact, a smile doesn't always mean the same, does it?

Of course not.

Tell me about the big break when you played in Longstreet.

Ah, that's it.

I must tell our audience that Bruce Lee had a bit part, or a supporting role, in the Longstreet *series and that his performance had an enormous effect on the audience. Why do you think this was?*

The title of that particular episode of *Longstreet* was "The Way of the Intercepting Fist." I think the successful ingredient in it was that I was *being* Bruce Lee.

Yourself.

Myself, right. And in doing that part I was able to just express myself. Like I say, I "honestly expressed myself" at that time. And, because of that, I received favorable mention in the *New York Times*, which said something like: "Bruce Lee, a Chinaman, who incidentally came off quite convincingly enough to earn himself a television series" and so on and so forth.

Can you remember the lines from that episode that you spoke that were written by Stirling Silliphant? The key lines?

He's one of my students, you know that?

Silliphant, too?

Yes [laughs].

Everybody's your student! But there were some lines in that episode that you spoke to Longstreet, who was played by James Franciscus. Those lines express your philosophy. I don't know if you can remember them.

Oh, I remember them. I said: "Empty your mind. Be formless, shapeless—like water. Now, you put water into a cup, it becomes the cup. You put water into a bottle, it becomes the bottle. You put it in a teapot, it becomes the teapot. Now, water can flow or it can crash. Be water, my friend." Like that, you see?

I get the idea, and the power behind it. So, now, there's a pretty good chance that you'll get a TV series in the States called The Warrior? *Where you use the martial arts in a Western setting?*

Well, that was the original idea. I did *Longstreet* for Paramount, and Paramount wants me to be in a television series. On the other hand, Warner Brothers wants me to be in another television series. But both of them, I think, want me to be in a *modernized* type of a thing. They think that the Western idea is out, whereas I want to do the Western. How else can you justify all of this punching and kicking and violence, except in that period of the West? Nowadays you don't go around on the street kicking people or punching people, because if you do [someone will simply pull out a gun and]—BANG! That's it. I mean, I don't care how good in martial arts you are, you're not going to stop a bullet.

But this is true also of the Chinese dramas, which are mainly costume dramas. They're all full of blood and gore over here in Hong Kong.

Unfortunately, that is often the case. You see, I hope that a picture that I am in would explain why the violence was done, whether right or wrong or whatever. Unfortunately, most of the pictures here in Hong Kong are done mainly just for the sake of violence. Guys fighting for thirty minutes straight, and getting stabbed fifty times.

I'm fascinated that you came back to Hong Kong on the verge of success in Hollywood—full of it, in fact—and then suddenly, on the strength of one picture, you have become a superstar. Now everybody knows you, you have to change your phone number, and you get mobbed in the streets. Now what are you going to do? Are you going to be able to live in both worlds? Are you going to be a superstar here, or one in the States? Or both?

Let me say this. First of all, the word *superstar* really turns me off, and I'll tell you why. The word *star* is an illusion; it's something that the public calls you. Rather, one should look upon oneself as an *actor*. I mean, I would be very pleased if somebody said, "Hey, man, you are a *super actor*!" It is much better than *super "star."*

Yes, but you've got to admit that you are a superstar, if you're going to give me the truth!

I am now honestly saying this: Yes, I have been very successful, but I do not look upon myself as a star. I really don't. Believe me, man, when I say it.

All right. So, what are you going to do? Let's get back to the question: are you going to stay in Hong Kong and be famous, or are you going to go back to the United States and be famous, or are you going to try to have your cake and eat it, too?

I am going to do both because, you see, I have already made up my mind that in the United States something about the Oriental, I mean the *true* Oriental, should be shown.

Hollywood sure as heck hasn't!

You better believe it. It's always the pigtail and bouncing around going "chop-chop," you know? And I think that's very, very out of date.

Is it true that the first job you had was being cast as Charlie Chan's "Number One Son"?

Yeah, "Number One Son" [laughs].

But they never made the movie?

No, they were going to make it into a new "Chinese James Bond" type of a thing: "Now that *Old Man* Chan is dead—Charlie is dead—so his son is carrying on."

But they didn't do that.

No. *Batman* came along. And then everything started to go into that kind of a thing.

Like The Green Hornet?

Right. By the way, I did a really terrible job in that, I have to say.

Really? You didn't like yourself in The Green Hornet?

Oh, no.

Let me ask you about the problems that you face as a Chinese hero in an "American" series. Have people in the industry come up and said: "Well, we don't know how the audience is going to take a non-American hero"?

Such questions have been raised. In fact, that issue is being discussed right now, and that is why *The Warrior* is probably not going to be on. Because, unfortunately, such things do exist in this world. In certain parts of the country, they think that business-wise it's a risk. And I don't blame them. I don't blame them. It's the same way in Hong Kong: if a foreigner came and became a star, if I were the man with the money, I probably would have my own worry of whether or not the acceptance would be there. But that's all right. If you honestly express yourself, it doesn't matter, because you will be successful.

How about the other side of the coin? You're fairly hip and fairly Americanized. Is it possible that you are "too Western" for some of your Asian audiences?

I have been criticized for that.

You have?

Oh, definitely. Let me say this: When I do the Chinese films, I will try my best not to be as "American" as I have been for the last twelve years in the States. But when I go back to the States, it seems to be the other way around.

You're too exotic?

Yeah. They're trying to get me to do too many things that are really for the sake of being exotic.

When you live in both worlds, it brings its problems as well as its advantages. And you've got both. Now let me ask you: has the change in attitude on the part of the Nixon administration toward China helped your chances of starring in an American TV series?

Well, first of all, this [American television series offer] happened before that. But I do think that Chinese things will be quite interesting for the next few years. I mean, I'm *not* politically inclined toward anything.

I understand that, but I was just wondering.

Once the opening of China happens, it will bring more *understanding*. And maybe in the contrast and comparison some new thing might grow. It is a very rich period to be in. I mean, for example, if I had been born 40 years ago, and if I had thought, "Boy, I'm going to star in a movie or star in a television series in America!"—well, that would have been a vague dream. But I think that right now, it may be possible.

Do you still think of yourself as "Chinese," or do you ever think of yourself as "North American"?

You know how I like to think of myself? As a *human being*. Because, and I don't want to sound like "As Confucius says," but under the sky, under the heavens, there is but *one family*. It just so happens that people are different.

Part II

Pierre Berton Reflects on Interviewing Bruce Lee

There was a sense of the unexpected in this interview.

What follows is an interview conducted with world-renowned Canadian author, commentator, lecturer, television personality, and journalist Pierre Berton, who was fortunate enough to conduct the only video interview with Bruce Lee that has survived the ravages of time. The video has caused something of a sensation in the martial arts world, as it represents the only time that Bruce Lee the man, as opposed to Bruce Lee the actor, was ever captured on film.

But how did Pierre Berton learn of Bruce Lee? What impact did Bruce Lee have in a television studio seated behind a desk—as opposed to appearing in front of his martial art students or on the big screen? Mr. Berton's answers to these and other questions are of immense historical interest from the perspective of his major role in preserving a unique facet of martial arts heritage.

Mr. Berton, can you give us some background on your interview with Bruce Lee? How did it come about? How did you first hear about him?

I didn't hear about Bruce Lee until I reached Hong Kong. The staff for my television show precedes me wherever I go—or at least they did in those days. They looked up possible subjects for me to interview, and Bruce Lee was one of them. And it seemed to me that he would make a good interview because, although he was not known in Canada, he was one of the best-known people at the moment in Hong Kong. His first

Chinese-language film had just been released, and it was the biggest box-office smash in Hong Kong history. He was, in short, a superstar—a word he didn't himself like very much. So, I interviewed him for half an hour, uncut, in the studio, and liked him very much.

You were the first North American journalist to sense the significance of this young man. What was it about him that made you think that there was a "story" here?

We traveled to Hong Kong to get a feeling about Hong Kong through various people we would interview. The enormous excitement over Bruce Lee, the fact that he was being literally mobbed in the streets, indicated that he would make a very good subject for the program. And then, as they always did, my staff did research for me—about 40 pages of close-spaced typing—so that by the time I got in front of the cameras with Bruce Lee, I knew quite a bit about him.

You mentioned that the interview ran about thirty minutes, with some pauses for commercial breaks. Did Bruce make any comments to you after the broadcast or during the breaks that you recall?

The thing about Bruce Lee at that time was that he had just been rocketed to stardom. It was not a word that he liked; he liked to be called an "actor" but not a "star." He talked a bit about that on the program and also off camera. He was obviously excited by what had happened to him, and I don't think that he had quite grasped the importance or the size of the excitement that was surrounding him. He had to change his telephone number right away, for instance. People were really after his autograph. The crew was as excited as he was—this sudden new superstar had entered the studio and was going to talk about himself.

In the interview, you, a Canadian, a westerner, came off as very well versed in Asian philosophy, which seemed to impress Bruce. What components of Bruce's philosophy impressed you the most?

He talked a lot about philosophy. He was really into it at that time, and he was trying to explain to me what we later learned partially from the television series called *Kung Fu*, which made "kung fu" one of the best-known phrases in the language along with names like jujitsu and judo and karate and all those things that were coming up. He was trying to explain what he was doing in philosophical terms as well as in action terms.

What were your overall impressions of Bruce Lee as a result of having spoken with him that day?

Bruce Lee was a very modest guy. He didn't, as I said, want to be called a "star." It turned him off to be called an instant superstar. He said to me, "I would be very pleased if somebody said, 'Hey, man, you're a super actor!'" But he said, "The word *star*, man, that's an illusion." He had a great deal of wit; he was a funny guy—in a sense. He was funny on the program: not so much that he told jokes—he didn't—but just the way he said things.

Also, and I think this is the most important impression that's remained with me about Bruce Lee, he was certainly the most intense character I have ever met on television, and I have interviewed at least 2,000 people for half an hour at a time. This guy was like a coiled spring! He would demonstrate with his fists or his hands these lightning moves, which astonished me. He could dart out with a fist or an arm and come within a millimeter of your face without touching you—which impressed me too. But he was quite clearly on top of his craft. That is to say, he wasn't like a Steven Seagal, or a Jean-Claude Van Damme, or any of these new characters that come along. He had developed an intense attitude toward what he did. He was very proud of what he did. He was very proud that he could teach it and that he had taught people like James Coburn. He was proud of the fact that he was an Asian. He was proud of the fact that for the first time, he thought, he wasn't going to be the usual stereotyped comic Chinese, that there was a real reason for him to be there. He had played Kato to the Green Hornet as a sort of subsidiary role rather like Lothar in the *Mandrake the Magician* comic strips or Tonto on *The Lone Ranger*. But now, and this is one of the tragic and ironic things about him, he hoped that they would buy his new series that he was pitching in Hollywood, which was going to be called *The Warrior* and was about an Oriental with kung fu skills in the Old West, and that he would be the star lead—the first Oriental to have a lead in anything. Even Charlie Chan was played by a white man! The ironic thing, of course, was that they bought the series but put somebody else in the title role who was white and then made him up to look Chinese, or rather to look "half-Chinese." I think that would undoubtedly have embittered him, although it hadn't happened when I started interviewing him.

How do you think Bruce Lee viewed his talent?

He thought of what he did as art. It wasn't a game, it wasn't a way to make money, it wasn't a gimmick—it was a form of art, and I think he brought it to that level. I got that great strong feeling that, although this was a witty man who talked in North American slang and who had been some time in the States, and who didn't sound like a Chinese philosopher, all the same, he was bringing a new kind of attitude to an old kind of unarmed combat.

The Longstreet *television episode that you cited in your interview was entitled "The Way of the Intercepting Fist," which is the English translation of the martial art that Bruce Lee created called* jeet kune do. *He said that the reason he was able to have such an impact on the audience in that episode was that he was "being Bruce Lee": in other words, honestly expressing himself and explaining the key tenets of his art as only the founder of such an art could. Did you see that episode prior to interviewing him?*

I didn't, but of course I knew about it because one of my researchers had spent considerable time with Bruce Lee finding out all about him so that I wouldn't look like a dummy [laughs] when I interviewed him! I was given quite a lot of information about him and used it in my interview.

How would you rate this interview, in terms of its impact and public interest, in comparison with others you've conducted?

This was a good interview. You get some bad ones and you get some good ones. You also get some that are unexpected. There was a sense, I think, of the unexpected in this interview, because until he came on the air, I didn't know whether he was a guy who was going to be glib about the martial arts or a guy who really believed in it. And he came across to me, and I think to the audience, as a guy who was sincere and who considered himself an artist—and with good reason. You know, he was an *educated* man; he wasn't a dummy. He'd been to university, and he had a philosophy about action, and he was trying to explain it, and I think he did explain it on the program.

Bruce Lee still holds a fascination to people all over the world. He's still appearing on magazine covers more than two decades since his passing, television shows feature biographies on him, and so on. What do you think the reasons are for his continued popularity?

I think it's the James Dean Syndrome, to a great extent, that explains the enormous cult that's built around him. But you can't have the James Dean Syndrome unless you have a James Dean style of actor. His sudden death, of course, increased the interest in him, but if he had been a journeyman or an average guy, then that would not have worked. It worked because he showed so much promise, as James Dean did. Lee had so much going for him. And he had created a character that was really himself, and he came across as himself, I think, in his films and certainly in my television interview. He wasn't a phony, in other words. He was *real*. He was real, and he was good at what he did, and what he did was *exotic*. So that when he died so suddenly, it added to what was really a myth or a mystery. He is certainly now a man of mythic proportions, and he seemed to be going that way even then.

*To diverge somewhat for a moment, what were your thoughts on
Hong Kong?*

I like Hong Kong. I've been to Singapore, which I find a
dreadfully boring town and a repressive one. The thing
I like about Hong Kong is that it's "high, wide, and
handsome." It's crowded, it's noisy, people jostle one
another, it's a moneymaking town, it's jammed, it's
raucous, and it's everything else, but I find it
stimulating and exciting. I love Hong Kong. I've been
there two or three times, and I enjoy it every time I go.

Was Bruce Lee your first exposure to the martial arts?

I don't think I'd ever heard of the martial arts before.
Well, I'd heard of jujitsu, and I'd heard of judo. I don't
think I'd even heard of karate, which had come in then.
These are Japanese martial arts. I had not heard
certainly of *gung fu*; that name did not register with
me. None of this registered with me until this first
meeting with Bruce Lee. Although, I did know there
were a lot of what they call "Chinese boxing" films
turned out by Hong Kong. When I was in Egypt in
Cairo, every movie theater seemed to have a "Chinese
boxing" film in it. I didn't know what the hell they
were about; I never went to see any of them. But Bruce
Lee raised that rather low profile, and I think he raised
it to the state of something it hadn't been before. And
that helped make the various martial arts, including his,

much more acceptable and interesting to the Western world.

What was the general reaction of the Hong Kong people to Bruce Lee at that time?

The entire Hong Kong people were crazy about Bruce Lee! I think one of the things they liked about him was that this guy who had played a sort of subservient role as Kato in *The Green Hornet* was now his own man. And I think that was one of the secrets of the success of that first film, which was released in this country as *Fists of Fury*. That film showed a different kind of Kato-like person to the Hong Kongese. Lee's whole personality, which was exciting, dramatic, and engaging, came across, so that they were able to do more than simply understand him: they were able to be *with* him. At any rate, the results were there to be seen on the street; he was surrounded by a mob wherever he went. He was quite clearly the *superstar*, whether he wanted to be or not.

In conclusion, then, what [impression] did your thirty-minute interview with Bruce Lee on December 9 of 1971 leave you with?

I was left with the impression that there was nothing clumsy about Bruce Lee. He was elegant and precise. I remember thinking about the precision with which he moved those fists and the balletlike movements of his body, which he was able to twist around. He was in wonderful shape. He was like a ballet dancer in many ways, and his art was similar to the art of a ballet dancer, and you see that to this very day in his films. We used to go down and watch the old and young Chinese practicing their tai chi, moving very slowly in unison in the park every morning. I think this is part of the Hong Kong world—these slow, controlled movements. I have a daughter who lives in Asia, and she's picked this up, half an hour a day. I think that's one of the arts of the East that has been taken over by the West, I hope successfully. It's slow motion. Lee moved sometimes as a man in slow motion in the movies, although he could be very quick when he wanted to. But he was certainly the equal of a ballet master when it came to the art of self-expression.

Part III

BRUCE LEE IN CONVERSATION WITH TED THOMAS

There is no such thing as an
effective segment of a totality.

In 1971, British broadcaster Ted Thomas owned a small dubbing company in Hong Kong. The Hong Kong movie industry was certainly "behind the times" when it came to producing films that would attract a worldwide audience, but his company made decent money dubbing the various Chinese films into English for limited distribution. And then a man named Bruce Lee came to town, and the Hong Kong film industry would never again be the same.

Lee's impact was akin to that of a meteorite smashing into Earth. On the strength of his talent alone, not only were Chinese films accepted into the global market, but also an unprecedented demand for them arose. Thomas was there when it happened—before, during, and after—and therefore he has a tremendous perspective on Bruce Lee's impact. As a news reporter for Radio Hong Kong, Thomas was also one of the few people to have grounds to interview Bruce Lee. And that he did, in a small commissary on the back lot of Golden Harvest Studios shortly after the release of Lee's first film, *The Big Boss* (released in North America as *Fists of Fury*).

As a screen tough guy, you're going to have to suffer what all movie heroes suffer: exhibitionists and nuts challenging you to fight. It has already started to happen, hasn't it?

Yes, it has.

How do you deal with it?

When I first learned martial art, I too challenged many established instructors. And, of course, some others have challenged me also. But what I have learned is that challenging means one thing and that is: What is your reaction to it? How does it get you? If you are secure within yourself, you treat it very lightly because you ask yourself: Am I really afraid of that man? Do I have any doubts that he might get me? And if I do not have such doubts and such feelings, then I would certainly treat it very lightly, just as if today the rain is coming down very strong, but tomorrow, baby, the sun is going to come out again. It's like that type of a thing.

Of course, they can't lose by challenging you; even if they lose the fight, they get the publicity of being a guy who actually fought you.

Well, let's face it, in Hong Kong today, can you have a fight? I mean a "no-holds-barred" fight? Is it a legal thing? It isn't, is it? And for me, a lot of things, like people challenging me, I am *always* the last to know. I am always the last to know, man. I always find out from newspapers, from reporters, before I personally know what the hell is happening.

Bruce, you were teaching the martial arts in the United States and two of your students were Steve McQueen and James Coburn. Did you find them tough people, the way they are portrayed on the screen?

First of all, James Coburn is not a fighter—a "lover," yes! [laughs] He is really a super nice guy. Not only that, but he is also a very peaceful man. He learns martial art because he finds that it is like a mirror to reflect himself. I personally believe that all types of knowledge are ultimately self-knowledge. And that is what he is after. Now, Steve is very uptight. Steve is very highly strung. He could be a very good martial artist. I hope that martial art will cool him down a little bit, maybe make him a little bit more mellow and more peaceful—like Jim [laughs].

Did Steve McQueen's time with you achieve that? Did you feel that he perhaps learned something from you?

No, not yet. First, because of shooting schedules and all that, he cannot have lessons on a regular basis. And, second, he is still on the level of regarding it as an *excitement*—like his motorcycle and his sports car—some form of release of his anger, or whatever you name it.

Bruce, how much of your screen personality is really you? I mean, you teach martial arts, so you're obviously very good at it. But, of course, teachers are not always the best exponents or practitioners.

Right.

Are you able to "take care" of yourself, would you say?

I will answer it first of all with a joke, if you don't mind. All the time, people come up and say, "Bruce, are you *really* that good?" I say, "Well, if I tell you I'm good, probably you will say that I'm boasting. But if I tell you I'm not good, you'll know I'm lying." All right, going back to being truthful with you, let's just put it this way: I have no fear of an opponent in front of me. I'm very self-sufficient, and they do not bother me. And, should I fight—should I do anything—I have made up my mind that, baby, you had better kill me before [I get you].

In The Big Boss *you play a man who is very slow to anger. He's shy, decadent. He even stays out of fights in the early scenes because of a promise he made to his mother. Is that a little bit like you, or is this just a screen personality?*

This is definitely a screen personality, because as a person, one thing that I have definitely learned in my life—a life of self-examination, self-peeling bit by bit, day by day—is that I do have a bad temper . . . a violent temper, in fact. So, that is definitely a screen personality, some person I am portraying, and not Bruce Lee—as he is.

As well as being a certainly successful film in terms of finance— The Big Boss *grossed more than any other picture in Hong Kong—it also shows some very explicit sex scenes, doesn't it? What's your reaction to being in bed with a lovely young movie star in front of the whole studio crew? Does it intimidate you?*

Well, it certainly would *not intimidate* me, I can tell you that! It's all right as long as the script justifies it. But I definitely do not agree with putting something in there just for the heck of it, because that would be exploitation. For instance, when I first started shooting *The Big Boss*, the first question they asked me was: How many thousands of feet of film is [your fight scene] going to be? My first question was: First of all, *why* do I start fighting? You see what I'm saying?

You were referring to your character's motivation.

Definitely. It seems to be the thing now to go for sex and blood just merely for the sake of sex, and merely for the sake of blood.

May I ask you a question that's been puzzling me ever since I saw the film?

Sure.

At the stage where you decide you're going to get revenge and, obviously, leading up to the climax, you suddenly decide to go off and make love to a girlfriend in the bordello. Now, what's the motivation behind that?

Well, that was a suggestion of the director's, the hero being such a simple man, and all of a sudden making up his mind that he's going to go and either kill or be killed. It's kind of a sudden thing. The thought just occurs to him that, well, doggone it, such is the basic need of a human being. I might as well enjoy it, before I kick the bucket. He had that type of an attitude. It was just an *occurrence*.

I think you would probably agree, Bruce, that the thing that's limited the appeal of Chinese films to Western audiences is that it's very unusual to find a Chinese actor who can act. And when I say that, I mean act in a manner that would make non-Chinese people pay money to see them.

Yeah.

You seem to have crossed that barrier. How do you think you've achieved it? Do you think it has to do with your time in the United States?

Oh, yes.

You studied there, didn't you?

Yes. It definitely has helped. When I first arrived, I did *The Green Hornet* television series back in '65, and as I looked around, I saw a lot of human beings. And as I looked at myself, I was the only *robot* there. I was not being myself. I was trying to accumulate external *security*, external *technique*—the way to move my arm, and so on—but never asking: what would Bruce Lee have done if such a thing had happened to me? When I look around, I always learn something, and that is: to always be yourself, express yourself, to have faith in yourself. Do not go out and look for a successful personality and duplicate him. That seems to me to be the prevalent thing happening in Hong Kong. They always copy mannerism; they never start from the very root of their being: that is, How can I be me?

You see, I've never believed in the word *star*. That's an illusion, man, something the public calls you. When you become successful, when you become famous, it's very, very easy to be blinded by all these happenings. Everybody comes up to you and it's "Mister Lee." If you have long hair, they'll say, "Hey, that's 'in'; that's the 'in' thing." But if you have no name, they will say, "Boy, look at the disgusting juvenile delinquent!" Too many people say "yes, yes, yes" to you all the time. As long as you realize what life is all about and that right now some game is happening—and realize that it is a game—fine and dandy. That's all right. But most people tend to be blinded by it, because if things are repeated too many times, you believe them. And that can become a habit.

The danger is believing the public impression of you.

That's right.

Your father warned you about the bad things in show business. Have you seen them, too? I mean, apart from the illusions?

Of course. Of course.

You seem to have come out of it remarkably well.

Well, let me put it this way. To be honest and all that, I'm not as bad as some of them, but I definitely am not saying that I am a *saint*, OK? [laughs]

Let's go back to the fighting, because, like it or not, it's the thing you are mainly identified with at this moment.

Unfortunately.

There are a number of styles of fighting—there's karate, judo, Chinese boxing—and it's a question you must have been asked hundreds of times before: Which do you think is the most effective?

My answer to that is this: There is no such thing as an effective *segment* of a *totality*. By that I mean, I personally do not believe in the word *style*. Because, unless there are human beings with three arms and four legs, unless we have another group of beings on Earth that are structurally different from us, there can be no different style of fighting. Why is that? Because we have two hands and two legs. The important thing is: how can we use them to the maximum? In terms of paths, they can be used in a straight line, curved line, up, round line. They might be slow, but depending on the circumstances, sometimes they might not be slow. And in terms of legs, you can kick up, straight—same thing, right? Physically, then, you have to ask yourself: How can I be so very well coordinated? Well, that means you have to be an athlete—using jogging and all those basic ingredients. After all that, you ask yourself: How can you honestly express yourself at that moment? And being yourself, when you punch, you really want to punch—not trying to punch because you want to avoid getting hit, but to really be in with it and express yourself. That to me is the most important thing. That is, how in the process of learning how to use my body can I come to understand myself?

The unfortunate thing is that there's boxing, which uses hands, and judo, which is throwing. I'm not putting them down, mind you. I am saying that it is a bad thing that because of styles, people are separated. They are not united together because styles became law. The original founder of every style started out with a hypothesis. But now it has become the gospel truth, and people who go into that style become the product of it. It doesn't matter who you are, how you are structured, how you are built, how you are made . . . it doesn't seem to matter. You just go in there and be that product. And that, to me, is not right.

Part IV

TED THOMAS REFLECTS ON INTERVIEWING BRUCE LEE

He knew he was unique; nobody like him had ever happened before.

British broadcaster Ted Thomas came to Hong Kong in the 1950s. He worked as a sports reporter for the *Hong Kong Standard* newspaper and, after two years, joined the government radio station, Radio Hong Kong (now RTHK), as a producer.

In time he came to host his own television talk show, entitled *On Camera*, on TVB, featuring interviews with virtually every celebrity who passed through Hong Kong in the late '60s and early '70s. It was during this period that the interview he recorded with Bruce Lee took place. Our session with Thomas took place twenty-two years after his interview with Lee, and yet Thomas's recollection of the interview and of the interviewee are as clear today as they were that fateful day in 1971 when he first switched on his microphone to interview the one and only Bruce Lee.

Mr. Thomas, when did you first hear of Bruce Lee?

We heard about him through a television series—a black-and-white television series—coming out of the United States called *The Green Hornet*. I note with some degree of amusement that these programs are now being rerun in Hong Kong, I believe on Star Television, so the wheel has turned full circle. It was sometime later that there was an announcement by the guy who left Shaw Brothers to set up Golden Harvest Film Studios, Raymond Chow, that he had signed up Bruce Lee to come to Hong Kong. At that time there were kung fu movies, of course, but they were starring people like David Lee and another man named Wong Yu from Taiwan, and they were the last to pretend that they were really kung fu fighters. They were, in fact, actors who did a bit of kung fu and thought it was all quite a joke.

How long after that did you actually meet Bruce?

I guess I met Bruce within a year of his coming to Hong Kong. I met him first of all in a dubbing studio. We were dubbing his voice, and Bruce wandered in with his hands in his pockets. We were watching a particular sequence where he was whirling around the double-headed club—the two clubs with the chain between. He was explaining that as he slammed them under his arm and around his back, he'd bruised himself under his armpits—pretty bad, in fact, around his rib cage. But it happened all the time, and he just accepted that. And he stripped off his shirt in front of everyone and showed us his bruises. He was always quite proud of his body. He was only a minuscule little chap but very, very well proportioned and very well muscled. The girls were all impressed.

Can you give us any background to the interview?

I don't remember the date of that particular interview, since I did many interviews with Bruce Lee over a period of time, both for newspapers and for radio and television. That one, I think, took place actually in the Golden Harvest Studios. He'd come in to do some dubbing that day.

What kind of a person was Bruce Lee?

Bruce was the sort of person who thought he could do absolutely everything. He was cocky, as most actors are. He would never have gotten where he was without having that tremendous self-confidence which seems to be a vital part of a successful acting career. He wasn't all that big-headed. Don't forget that he was making films where he was trying to reassert the authority and dignity of the Chinese race. He says one line in *The Big Boss* [actually Thomas means *Fist of Fury*, released in this country as *The Chinese Connection*]: "China is no longer the sick man of Asia!" They used to call China "the sick man of Asia." I think in Bruce's movies, it was the first time where you saw a tough Chinese overcoming and humiliating big, brutish Europeans, and that, in itself, was a change. Some of that carried over into Bruce's private life, although I must say I never saw him being threatening outside the studios.

But he did tend to be rather cocky, in particular with Europeans or British around, of course, because he was brought up in a British colony. And, at that time, the Chinese did tend to be second-class citizens. There were two completely different pay scales: if you were of overseas extraction, you got your rent paid, and you got your first-class passage to your own country and back, and you got your electricity and gas paid. Chinese people of the same talent didn't get any of these things.

You mentioned during the interview that Bruce was already beginning to receive "challenges" from various martial artists in Hong Kong. Do you recall any of these, and did he eventually decide to accept any?

Bruce was one of the first kung fu fighters who could really fight, who knew what it was all about and was quite prepared to take on people. And he did get a lot of challenges, but I don't ever remember his agreeing to take one on. I do remember discussing with him that the challenger "can't lose." I mean even if Bruce half killed him in a fight, the guy could say, "Well, I fought Bruce Lee." And if the guy got in a few lucky licks and broke Bruce's nose or something, then the guy was going to be a very, very important person and a very well-known person. So, Bruce was sensible enough to understand that even when people say, "Oh, he's a phony; he doesn't really know anything about kung fu," you've got to keep your lip buttoned and not fight back. As far as I know, he never actually accepted one of them, and I don't think that if he had, it would have been in his best interests.

Did you ever hear of any encounters where Bruce had to defend himself for real in Hong Kong?

No, although I did hear an anecdote that he was in a nightclub once and somebody said something to one of his friends which upset him and he was involved in a fight and half killed the guy but that it was all covered up by—and I do stress that this is a rumor—Raymond Chow, who had paid out a good deal of money to bury the whole thing. I don't think there was anything ever published about it.

How many times did you interview Bruce while he lived in Hong Kong?

Probably about a dozen times. Sometimes it was not as a formal interview; it would be in the rest room out at the studios. When I say "the rest room," I mean the Tea Shop, the canteen out at Golden Harvest Studios. We were going out there quite a lot. We were dubbing movies every weekend and sometimes two or three evenings a week. Bruce was shooting there, and between takes he liked to come into the dubbing studios. He tended, I think, to be more happy in the company of Europeans, or "westerners," than he was amongst the Chinese crews. He would "shoot the breeze" for a while. And he liked helping out in dubbing the bit parts; if we had a small characterization, Bruce would love trying his hand at it.

What's happened to those interviews?

I've no idea. That was over twenty years ago. Rᴛʜᴋ (Radio/Television Hong Kong) broadcast them, and I wrote about them in newspapers. I've no idea if they're still there. They're all on microfiche nowadays, so it wouldn't be too difficult to do cross-references. But of course, after he died, everybody in the world was claiming that they'd interviewed him, and so it would probably be among all those.

You mentioned in a prior conversation that you once engaged in some playful sparring with Bruce and inadvertently clipped him in the mouth with a right hook. Obviously the two of you were fooling around at the time, but all in all, how would you assess his skills as a martial artist?

Well, it wasn't really playful sparring. I was having an argument with Bruce about the fact that, in my view, a gifted or talented and really agile Western boxer would

51

always beat any martial artist. I said this because many years before in Manila, I had witnessed a fight between a boxer and what was then called a judo expert, or a jujitsu expert, and the whole competition—which involved five or six different fights—ended up exactly the same: the martial artists were laid out in every case. Whether that was because they weren't particularly good judo experts or the boxers were exceptionally good, I don't know. Bruce, of course, loved to play around and said, "Hit me—I bet you can't hit me." So, I sort of swung at him with a left first of all, because that's normally what a boxer would be looking for. A left hand tends to be the first shot in most boxers' armory. As he jerked his head away to the right—his left, my right—I caught him with a right, and while I didn't intend to hurt him, it split his lip. I can't say that he was very pleased about it [laughs]. All he said was, "Yeah, you'd be easy to hit; you drop your left shoulder when you hit with your right arm," which is quite true: I do and did at that time. But he never got angry about it. When we used to sort of spar around with open hands as boxers do, with the flat of the hands and hitting with the edge of the hand or slapping, he was never one of these people that let it get out of hand or who got angry.

Did you ever have an opportunity to witness Bruce work out?

Yes, lots of times. He favored running very much. He didn't lift particularly heavy weights, or at least he didn't when I saw him. He had all kinds of peculiar exercises of his own which I never understood with my limited knowledge of the sort of training needs that someone like Bruce would have. I would have thought that persistent training, like running, and arm exercises, were what he would have followed most routinely. He was also quite a good gymnast. He could spring forward and stand on his hands and once told me that he could do a standing somersault flip, but I never actually saw him do it. He came across as a very fit person who took his body very seriously.

You helped to dub some English-language voices onto a few of his films.

Actually I did more than help dub the English voices. I was involved in writing scripts and directing, and I owned the dubbing company. We did *The Big Boss* and the second one, and I think we did part of one other that they were trying to stitch together after Bruce had died. I remember years later being in Hong Kong and one of our dubbers, Ian Wilson, telephoning me from New York and saying, "You're not going to believe this, Ted, but we're watching late-night movies in the Plaza Hotel in New York and on comes Bruce Lee, and whose voice do you think is coming out of Bruce Lee? It's yours!"

Describe your relationship with Bruce Lee from 1971 up until his passing in 1973. Was it jovial, serious, friendly, strained?

It's difficult to describe the relationship with Bruce. I'm tempted to say we were friends. We certainly weren't "strained." I'll take your adjectives for a start: We were "jovial," yes; I think we were quite jovial. We used to jostle and kid each other about talents, different talents. I don't think we ever got "serious." I think we were "friendly" as much as we knew each other. We'd stop for a chat whenever we passed on the street or I was on the set or when he was in my dubbing studio. I don't think it was ever "strained." I think it was always a relationship where Bruce felt that he could let his hair down a bit with a *gwei-lo* [literally, a "foreign devil"] who wasn't a threat to him in any way.

What do you think Bruce was trying to accomplish with his films?

Bruce talked a lot about philosophical aims and how to bring people together and how "nation shall speak to nation." He knew he could do that with films. He knew he was unique; nobody like him had ever happened before. I think what he did achieve, whether he intended to or not—he gave back the Chinese a great deal of dignity in their lives. Previously, they'd always been portrayed as obsequious—always-grinning waiters, personal servants. For the first time, Bruce was a tough-guy Chinese without being a gangster, just a guy who at some point in his life said, "That's enough; I'm not taking any more of it."

Did your having known Bruce Lee leave any impact on you personally?

Well, of course, the main thing was his death. At that time I was the chief of the Royal Hong Kong Police Public Relations Bureau, which I'd help to set up. It was at a time when cops were being arrested for corruption at an alarming rate. The government decided they would have to do something about it, and I was brought in to improve the police public relations. I had a standing order that if anything happened to anybody who was well known, even though I had a staff of about 60, I was to be telephoned. Whether there had been a murder or a rape or a suicide or a robbery that involved a well-known figure in the government or a well-known visitor from other parts, I was to be told.

On the night that Bruce was discovered dead, I was having dinner with the commissioner of police, Charles Suttcliffe, a rather blunt Yorkshireman, and I was called to the phone by my Number Two and informed that Bruce Lee had committed suicide. That was the first story we got. They thought it was an overdose of some pills and that this had happened in the garden of his home. I thought this a bit strange. If you were going to commit suicide, you wouldn't want to do it in the garden of your own home, with all of the distress that would bring to your family. I said I better go and find out what was happening, because I knew that all the newspapers in the world would be on to us about it.

We discovered that it had been a false report. The next day after the first news, it did come out that he had been discovered up in the apartment. He had had a headache and he'd gone to bed, taken some medication, and died in that bed. That was the official story, and that's the story that people still tend to describe. As far as I know, Bruce never did any drugs. He looked after himself pretty well; he wasn't a drinker or anything.

Why do you think Bruce Lee is still revered in so many parts of the world today?

I think for the fact that he has become an icon for the reasons that we've already discussed.

What did Bruce Lee stand for?

I suppose a tough self-sufficiency. An inability to take any shit from anyone.

Since you knew him rather well, what image of Bruce comes to your mind most readily?

He was quite a decent chap, basically. He wasn't as vain as most actors I've met. He was, as far as I know, always ready to help a friend, and he was very, very generous to his friends in giving his time and his advice and that sort of thing.

How do you think history will remember Bruce Lee?

I guess there will be a cult in the same way that there was a Rudolph Valentino cult. Valentino didn't make many movies, and neither did Bruce. But Bruce made *different* movies, and they did produce an answer to what Raymond Chow had said when he first left Run Run Shaw—then the biggest moviemaker in the Far East: that "good-quality movies would sell." Raymond's own background is also worth looking into. When I first met him, he was, I think, a clerk at the United States Information Service in the U.S. Consulate and he'd gone to work for Run Run Shaw and discovered that things there were not to his liking. So, he set up his own film company, Golden Harvest, and has done an excellent job of rebuilding or building up the Asian movie industry to a state where it is very successful. I should imagine that on the balance, Chinese movies make a lot more than movies in other languages. He upgraded the quality, and one of his great upgrades was having the perspicacity and being prescient enough to see that Bruce Lee was somebody who was going to be very, very spectacularly successful, and that people were going to relate to him. And Bruce will be, I think, remembered for being the first of the great action kung fu movie stars, and the man who made a Chinese hold up his head in the international scene and be proud of himself—which he was.

Part V

BRUCE LEE IN CONVERSATION WITH ALEX BEN BLOCK

*The thing is how to make good use of yourself—
and that's about it.*

In late summer of 1972, freelance writer Alex Ben Block made a long-distance phone call to Hong Kong. The man he called was Bruce Lee, then a thirty-one-year-old superstar in the Eastern world who was virtually unknown in the West. Block's intention was to interview Lee as part of a feature on the martial arts that was to be used in *Esquire* magazine.

Lee took the call on the set of his third film, *The Way of the Dragon* (the working title at the time being *Enter the Dragon*). It would prove to be a very significant interview, for in addition to offering exceptional autobiographical content, it is the last known in-depth interview ever granted by Bruce Lee.

You were born in San Francisco, I understand.

Right. I was born on November 27, 1940—Sagittarius!

And you moved to Hong Kong shortly after that?

Yes, when I was three months old.

Were you educated in Hong Kong?

Partly. I was educated in Hong Kong up until I was 18 years old. Then I moved back to the States and eventually attended the University of Washington in Seattle.

And what was your major?

Are you ready for it? *Philosophy*, man!

You were a child actor in Hong Kong?

Yes, I started acting when I was around six years old.

What kind of things did you do in these films?

Well, mainly *unimportant* things. Up until I was around 18 years old.

Is your father still alive?

No, my father passed away in 1965.

What was his name?

Lee Hoi Chuen.

Your father was fairly famous in the Chinese opera. Did you ever appear in any films with him?

No, not really. Chinese opera is a completely different thing. I never did like Chinese opera that much. I much rather liked to watch *The Lone Ranger*, you know? [laughs]

Was your mother in the theater too?

No, she wasn't.

You make your films now in the Chinese language?

In Mandarin, yes.

How many languages do you speak?

Cantonese, English, and a little bit of Mandarin.

So, what do you feel your nationality is?

"American," of course, because I hold a U.S. passport. And as soon as I finish with all these films in Hong Kong, I would like to move back to the States and just stay there.

How tall are you?

Five-seven and a half.

And your weight?

One-forty.

You don't have to answer this next question if you don't want to, but what is your religion?

None whatsoever.

None? Do you believe in "God"?

To be perfectly frank, I really do not.

Did you ever have any other jobs besides being an actor?

Yes, I was teaching martial art.

In the United States?

Yes, I had three schools: one in Oakland, one in Seattle, and one in Los Angeles. And then later on I closed them and just taught private lessons.

And you call your martial art jeet kune do, *correct?*

Yes. Exactly.

Were your schools called the "Jeet Kune Do Schools"?

Actually, I do not believe in "schools." More and more, I believe in the fact that you have two hands and two legs, and the thing is how to make good use of yourself—and that's about it. "Styles" kind of restrict you to only one way of doing it and therefore limit your human capacity.

You once were quoted as saying: "Man, the living creature, the creating individual, is always more important than any established style." Do you mean by this that one must change one's style all the time in the martial arts?

No. I mean this: we are always in a learning process, whereas a "style" is a concluded, established, solidified something. You cannot do that, because you learn every day as you grow older.

You've also been quoted as saying that there is "no difference between a Japanese martial artist and a Chinese martial artist who come to jeet kune do." *Could you explain this?*

Many people will come to an instructor, but most of them say, "What is the truth? Would you hand it over to me?" So, typically, one instructor would say, "I'll give you my *Japanese way* of doing it." And another guy would say, "I'll give you the *Chinese way* of doing it." But to me that's all baloney. Nationalities don't mean anything. There are different approaches, you know? But each person must not be limited to one approach. We must aproach it with our own self, for art is the expression of one's own self, whereas if you go to a Japanese style, then you are expressing the Japanese style; you are not expressing yourself.

You've also said that "life is a constant process of relating," in talking about jeet kune do. *What do you mean by that?*

Well, for instance, when I see a Japanese martial artist, I can see the advantage and the disadvantage of his style. In that sense, I am relating to him. Man is living in a relationship, and in relationship we grow.

Doesn't this philosophy that you have go against much of what is taught in the martial arts by the more orthodox instructors?

Yes, because most of them are so doggone stubborn. Their approach to martial art is something like, "Well, 200 hundred years ago it was taught like this!" But to maintain that type of attitude today means that you've had it! You would still be back there; you will never grow, because learning is a *discovering* thing. It's a constant discovery, whereas if we follow the old method, it is simply a continuous repetition of what was being handed down several hundred years ago.

How many hours a week do you spend practicing jeet kune do?

I average around two hours a day.

How old were you when you began studying the martial arts?

I was thirteen years old.

Did you study under a famous teacher?

I studied under Yip Man. He was my instructor in a Chinese martial art.

And what style of the martial arts was that?

The style is called *wing chun*.

And is that a Chinese form of karate?

Actually you could not call it "a Chinese form of karate," because karate came into existence *after* Chinese *gung fu*, and it was Chinese *gung fu* that I was studying.

So it was a form of kung fu?

Yes. All these [martial arts], like karate, came after Chinese *gung fu*.

Are you married?

Oh, yeah, definitely. I have two kids.

How long have you been married?

I've been married now for around nine years.

What is your wife's name?

Linda.

And is Linda Chinese or American?

She's American.

Didn't you live in Los Angeles the last time you lived in the United States?

Yes, I lived in Los Angeles from 1965 until 1971.

Who was your agent in Los Angeles?

I really didn't have an agent in the sense that most actors have agents. It was through my teaching that I got my jobs. I was teaching people like James Coburn, Stirling Silliphant, Steve McQueen, and all those guys.

You were teaching them jeet kune do?

Yes.

And this was when you were acting, or before?

It was both during and before.

Were they good pupils?

Yeah. They were all right.

What are your hobbies? What do you do to relax?

Work! And work out. And doing the things that I want, like making movies and things like that.

You've mentioned that at age eighteen you returned to the United States. What year was this, and what part of the States?

I returned to the United States in 1959. I went to San Francisco first, and then I went up to Seattle.

And it was in Seattle that you went to school. When did you become a professional actor?

That's a very funny story, because when I went back to the States, I really didn't think of continuing my career in films. I mean, here I am, a Chinese, and—I don't mean this to sound prejudiced or anything, but—in realistic thinking, how many times in [Western] films is a Chinese required? And when he is required, it is always branded as the typical "tung-de-de-lung-lung, dung, dung, dung." So, I said, "To hell with it." However, in 1964, in Long Beach, at the International Karate Tournament I gave a demonstration, and William Dozier saw it. He was doing the *Batman* TV series at that time. He signed me up, and I did *The Green Hornet*, and then later I went on and did *Longstreet*.

How long did The Green Hornet *series last?*

It lasted for one season.

And then it went into great rerun success in the Orient. It did much better there than it did in this country, didn't it?

In a way, it established me here in Hong Kong.

In 1969 you gave a highly publicized TV demonstration in Hong Kong. What did you do in this demonstration that impressed so many people?

That television appearance was in 1970. In the demonstration I had a person dangle five one-inch boards in the air, and I side-kicked them and broke four of them. It is much easier to break boards that are held securely by a person using two arms. It is very difficult to do when the boards are suspended in the air.

Had you already signed the contract to make your first film at this point?

No, I had not signed any contracts at this point.

And then you returned to the States and did some episodes of Longstreet?

Did you see the one in which I taught James Franciscus?

No, I didn't. I've heard about it, though.

When you get a chance, ask Paramount to show it to you, because it is worth seeing. Stirling Silliphant and I sat down and wrote that episode together. That was the premiere episode. In fact the name of it was "The Way of the Intercepting Fist." [This is the literal translation of *jeet kune do*.] The people at Paramount asked me to go back and do a television series. And Warner Brothers was committed to working out a TV series for me as well. They were offering me twenty-five grand simply to *hold* me to do a television series, but I didn't really want to do it. Then I went back to Hong Kong in 1971 and did a movie called *The Big Boss*, and the damn thing just broke the all-time record.

The Big Boss *was produced by Raymond Chow and directed by Lo Wei?*

Yes.

How much did The Big Boss *cost to make, do you know?*

Very cheap.

What is "very cheap"?

Around five hundred thousand Hong Kong dollars, which is less than one hundred thousand U.S.

And how much did it make?

It grossed, in Hong Kong alone, around $500,000 U.S. All the time before that, Chinese flicks were considered kind of unrealistic. There was a lot of overacting and a lot of jumping around, and all in all, they lacked any degree of realism. So, I came back and I introduced some new elements into filmmaking here. For instance, when I kick, I really kick. Let me say this: ultimately, martial art is the expression of oneself.

And in your films, do you express yourself?

Yes, as honestly and as much as I can. I think my doing that helped to make this film a huge success.

Was The Big Boss *filmed in Hong Kong, too?*

No, it was filmed in Bangkok. And then my next film, *Fist of Fury*, came out—and it broke the record set by my first film by over one million dollars.

Was Raymond Chow again the producer and Lo Wei again the director on Fist of Fury?

Ah, yes.

How much did Fist of Fury *cost to make?*

> *Fist of Fury* cost around eight hundred thousand Hong
> Kong dollars, which is under two hundred thousand
> U.S. dollars.

And how much did it gross?

> It has grossed close to one million dollars U.S.—in
> Hong Kong alone.

Where else will it play besides Hong Kong?

> Well, *The Big Boss*, my first Chinese film, broke the all-
> time record in Hong Kong and Singapore. And in
> Thailand and Singapore right now *Fist of Fury* is doing
> the same. And the film that I'm working on now, while
> it has not yet been released, I have every inch of
> confidence is going to break the records set by the
> previous two films.

You are presently working on your third film?

> Yes. In fact, we're shooting today on location. The
> picture is called *Enter the Dragon*. [Later it would be
> retitled *The Way of the Dragon* in Southeast Asia and
> released in North America as *Return of the Dragon*.] It is
> being produced by my company, and I am directing it.
> Do you know of Chuck Norris?

I've heard the name.

Well, he is also in it. And we shot in many locations in Rome.

What is the plot?

It is really a simple plot of a country boy going to a place where he cannot speak the language, but somehow he comes out on top because he—well, again, because he *honestly and simply expresses himself* [laughs] by "beating the hell out of 'em!"

Anyway, I've got to go now because my lunch break is over. And we have to start shooting. My producer has just said that I do not even have time to eat my lunch now [laughs].

Please answer just a couple of more questions for me. Will your films be dubbed into English?

Well, let me say this: Warner Brothers may be coproducing a film with us. [The film referred to here is Warner Brothers' smash hit *Enter the Dragon*, which began principal filming in February 1973.] And I am planning to do some films *strictly* in English. I really have a feeling that it's just a matter of time before the Chinese films reach the States, like the Italian flicks— or like a Clint Eastwood type of a thing.

In an article that I read in an American martial arts magazine it said that you have been challenged by a lot of people who want to make their reputation by "beating Bruce Lee." Is that still true?

Oh, yes. Every damn day. In fact, there's one who challenged me who later became a movie actor himself. There are actually companies here that are beginning to hire him. And, of course, he was punched out by somebody else: after the film they got into a fight. People challenge me, and certain fans of mine don't like it, so somebody else challenges the guy who challenged me!

Do you enjoy being an actor?

Yes, every inch of it, because it is my way of expressing myself. You know, it is quite phenomenal, too, in a way. I've heard that the word has come out over here that whoever can get me to sign a contract with another company will be getting, as a middleman, ten thousand dollars U.S.! Can you believe that? It's getting to the point where I don't even believe it myself!

How has your life changed? I understand you're a cult figure in Hong Kong. You're very famous there.

Well, it's changed in a sense that it's like I'm in jail.

Really? Like what?

Well, I'm like the monkey in the zoo. People come and look at me and things like that, but basically I like a simple life, and I like to joke a lot. But now I cannot speak as freely as I could before, because misinterpretation comes in.

Have you changed since you've gotten successful?

It hasn't changed me, basically because I know that in my [life], something simply happened which is breaking some records. It doesn't mean anything. It's just something that *happened*. I mean, it didn't give me any reason to think that I should be proud or that I'm any better than I ever was. I'm just the same, [laughs] the same damn old shit!

With regard to your lifestyle in Hong Kong, do you have your own home or do you live in an apartment?

I've just bought a beautiful house. I have to say, *that* change, you know, was most welcome.

How big a house did you buy?

Let's just say that it's very *comfortable*!

How many rooms does it have?

Upstairs there are six and downstairs there are three.

How much did it cost?

Well, let's not quote prices, shall we?

When you return to the United States, will you live in Los Angeles?

Yes, that's where I would live.

Do you still teach martial arts, or are you too busy now?

No, I couldn't teach martial art now because I have to work every day. In fact, listen, I've got to go and make a movie *now* [laughing]. My producer is using *jeet kune do* to kick the hell out of me right now!

On Enter the Dragon, *are you the director and the actor-star?*

Yes, I'm the actor, the director, the producer, the writer, and the whole bit.

You wrote it, too?

Yes, I screenplayed it.

When will this film be released?

It will be out probably by Chinese New Year.

Part VI

ALEX BEN BLOCK REFLECTS ON INTERVIEWING BRUCE LEE

I don't think there's been anyone in the last twenty-four years who can hold a candle to him.

A lex Ben Block is best known to people in North America as the editor of the *Hollywood Reporter*, a high-profile publication focusing on the entertainment industry in the United States. However, to Bruce Lee fans, the name Alex Ben Block holds even greater significance, for Alex wrote one of the first articles heralding the emergence of Bruce Lee as a major cinematic force in the Western world. This article, which was published by *Esquire* magazine in their August 1973 issue, gave birth to the first-ever biography of Bruce Lee in North America. It was called *The Legend of Bruce Lee*.

How did your interview with Bruce Lee come about?

I was a freelance writer in the early 1970s, living in New York City. I was researching a number of subjects. I was working for a rock-and-roll magazine called *Crawdaddy*, and I ended up writing an article for them about the martial arts. During the course of writing that article, a number of people said to me that the most interesting thing going on was that there was this actor, Bruce Lee, who had made a couple of films that were just released in the Orient which were becoming tremendously successful and were likely to be released here. He was quite a phenomenon with audiences. He was being mobbed by huge crowds in Hong Kong, and he was quite an exciting personality. During that period I had been writing to *Esquire* and suggesting story ideas. I got a call one day from an editor who said "OK, we'd like you to do a story, and the idea you suggested on Bruce Lee is the one we want." It was kind of out of the blue!

I contacted Bruce Lee through Warner Brothers and other contacts that I had. He was quite surprised, I believe, at the time, but he said, "Sure, I'll talk to you!" And we arranged a phone call. However, before that could happen I got a job that summer on a resort newspaper off the coast of New York. So, I was out on this little sandbar resort, putting out a newspaper for New Yorkers who wanted to suntan, during this phone call with Bruce Lee. And, unfortunately, I had problems with my tape recorder that day, and Bruce was very busy and harried and didn't have much time, but he gave me what time he could, and that interview later became the basis for the book *The Legend of Bruce Lee*.

Throughout the course of your interview, you cite an article that Bruce wrote in 1971 for a martial arts publication. What impressed you the most about that article?

During the period of research, when I started, I didn't know a great deal about the martial arts. Later on, inspired by Bruce Lee, I actually did study a martial art a little bit and got much more involved with it and studied it certainly philosophically over the years. But at the time, I didn't know a great deal about it.

What intrigued me was that martial arts was almost like a religion. People became very, very involved with it. It wasn't just physical exercise or physical culture, but rather it was a combination of physical, mental, and emotional, all wrapped together. And for the practitioners of these arts, many of which are ancient and have great traditions and have teachers who are much revered, these styles are so significant and such an important part of their life, that it's almost like a Catholic priest talking about being a Catholic, or a rabbi talking about being Jewish. This was very much a part of their being. And what Bruce Lee had said was, "I'm going to disregard all of that stuff, all of that old tradition, push it aside. But I'll take what I feel is the best of each of these different arts and I'll put it together and form my own philosophy," which, of course, he called *jeet kune do*. At the time, it was quite revolutionary.

I was a young man, and I was quite taken with how this young man was turning his whole world, the world that he knew and was known in, upside down and doing it in a way that he said was going to "revolutionize the world." Remember, this was 1972 that we did the interview, and we were still very much affected by what had happened in the '60s, when America really had gone through a revolution. And Bruce Lee and I, each in our own way, were a product of this period of great change, so it was very exciting for me to be able to talk to him about it.

When you interviewed other martial artists during the course of your research for The Legend of Bruce Lee, *what was the attitude toward Bruce that you experienced from these people?*

The attitude toward Bruce really depended upon the source. There were people who absolutely admired him. Of course, when someone dies that young who is such a wonderful person and had such a big influence, there are people who were very dedicated to him. And for those people it was a great tragedy. They talked about him like a lost leader, a great hero who had fallen much too early in his career. Of course, I also met other people who said, "This was some brash, wise-guy movie actor, and we didn't like him. He wanted to put down our style of martial arts. He wasn't someone who we admired; he was the opposite of that." So, within the martial arts there was this great dichotomy.

But what I was quite affected by, and I saw over a period of years, was that for many Asian Americans Bruce Lee marked a turning point. Asian Americans had felt prejudice, as Bruce Lee had felt prejudice when he came to America. Like many other minorities—the Asian Americans certainly weren't alone in this way— they had to work very hard to get any recognition. It seemed as if other people who had been in the culture longer had more access to opportunity than they did. What Bruce represented was the first Asian superstar in movies. He was truly a role model whom these people could accept and really take as a hero. And for many of the young people, not just Asians but also young African Americans or young minorities of all kinds, even for Caucasians who came from lower economic backgrounds, Bruce Lee was a hero. He represented someone who was able to break out of all of the things that seem to bind us in society and keep us from becoming a success, and truly rise above all that. Even after his death he remained a hero for many of those people.

Of course, he was incredibly exciting to watch on the screen and would literally jump out at you in his movies, and his movies were psychologically geared to make you feel total empathy with him. Before he fought or killed anybody, you felt, "My God! Do it, Bruce! You deserve to do it, because you've really built this thing up!" There was a real feeling about this guy that he was a hero and a role model, and although he had died like Jimmy Dean or Marilyn Monroe, I suppose he had achieved a kind of cult status that lived beyond his years.

I found it very exciting to talk to people and to travel around at my book signings, because people wanted to talk about him. They were excited about him, and he was truly a great hero for most of them. And, while there were some who really disliked him—in particular, in Hong Kong I found some people who just had bad things to say about him—for the most part people just felt that it was a tragedy that someone with such potential, with such talent, and with so much to give had died so young.

One of the other things you touched upon with these other martial artists in America is that when Bruce died, he died sort of at the crest of the wave that hit regarding martial arts films and martial arts awareness in this country generally. When most North Americans and Europeans were saying, "Hey, what was that?" Bruce was gone, with the result that the answer that came forth from various martial artists was: "What Bruce Lee did was simply martial arts—that's the magical thing about what he did—and I do martial arts too! Put me in a movie!" And they did, and for the past 22 years people have been watching these other martial artists in movies with greater or lesser success. But now there seems to be almost a backlash where they no longer want to see, for example, another Van Damme or another Chuck Norris. They seem to be coming back to Bruce Lee again. Why was he so different from these other martial artists?

First I would suggest that Bruce Lee unfortunately died before the "wave" hit and that he was responsible for the only meaningful wave of martial arts films. Later Jackie Chan and Chuck Norris had some success, but it was never on the level or with the intensity that Bruce Lee had. I think it's curious that even the people who put out the movies never really understood, in my opinion, what it was that was appealing about Bruce Lee.

I think what it was, really, was that he wasn't just about the fighting arts. He had a philosophy. He had a deep system of belief that he brought to everything he did. He wanted to deliver punches efficiently, but he also understood that you don't just punch people without having a reason. Some of the best parts of the movies he made, for me, weren't the fighting scenes, some of which could be a little hokey at times, but were the philosophy scenes where he talked to people and really got into it. But even with the fighting—and remember, Bruce also did his own choreography almost completely, and he choreographed others in the same movies he was in—he was not only a fighter but also a personality. He jumped off the screen. He was in your lap. You really got *caught up* in his movies.

Unfortunately there weren't that many of them, and some of them were rather crudely made, which makes it hard to go back now and follow it. But *Enter the Dragon* was a movie that really went beyond any movie in that genre before it, because he had this system of belief, and he had this great physique, and he had this idea, and he carried it forward. And he embodied a whole spirit. It wasn't just about punching people out. It was curious to me that, at the time that *Enter the Dragon* came out, it had a number of scenes where Bruce went to one of his mentors in a garden, an old man, and spoke to him about philosophy. As soon as the movie became a big hit, the first thing that Warner Brothers and the theater owners did was cut the movie shorter. One thing they cut out was all the philosophy. They left in all the fighting scenes. It just showed me that they had no comprehension of what had made these movies successful.

And then, of course, we saw this plethora of pathetic, terrible movies out of Hong Kong and Taiwan and other parts of the Orient and parts of America, where these pale imitators—some of who misspelled Bruce's name but made it sound phonetically the same—tried to adopt his style, thinking that the noises he made, or the moves he made, they could copy him. But he was the original.

You know, if you take a painting by Picasso and you try to paint a copy of it, it's not a painting by Picasso— it's a copy. It's not the same thing. It's not fresh. I don't believe that Bruce Lee, had he lived, would have repeated himself and made the same kinds of movies over and over. I think he would have evolved in his art and I think he would have evolved in his movies and that you would have seen change and growth in a very dynamic career. That was one of the sad things about his death. But the imitators really destroyed the genre that he created almost overnight. And, within a short time, martial arts movies, kung fu movies, karate movies—whatever you want to call them—became a kind of cultural joke. And to anybody who took movies seriously—grown-ups who wanted to go to quality movies—as soon as they saw that it was a martial arts movie, they wanted nothing to do with it. I think that had Bruce lived, that might not have been the case.

While I would assume that most of your peers would view martial arts films as a joke, it seems that with you there is a certain degree of reverence for Bruce's films.

I absolutely have reverence for Bruce's films, and I've collected most of them on video. He embodied something very special. He really did have an energy that came off the screen that very few individuals have. As with Clint Eastwood in his best movies or the late Steve McQueen in his best films, or occasionally a young actor who comes along, suddenly you forget you're in a movie, you forget you're in a theater, you forget everything except what's going on on that screen. You get all caught up with it. I think Bruce in his best moments did that. He also had a sense of humor, which is very important and something that those who followed him in martial arts movies seem to have forgotten. He liked to have a good joke; he liked to have a laugh. He was very human. He liked to have a girlfriend and buddies, and all of his movies usually involved crews of people that he would pal around with, whether they were members of a martial arts organization or people who worked in a restaurant with him, but they were people that he defended and who became, if not followers of his, like brothers of his.

Like extended family.

Right, like extended family. I think Bruce's films were full of that kind of warmth, and they conveyed something special. Were they great movies in the sense that the critics from the *New York Times* are going to say, "My God, this is a great movie!"? Absolutely not. But within the genre of action movies, Bruce had something special—and that is very, very hard to repeat, and that's why, I think, those films hold up.

What was your perception of Bruce before you interviewed him, and what was your perception after the interview?

Before I interviewed him, I assumed that he was sort of the typical "movie-star" type and that he was going to be some sort of glib guy, more shallow than a person with depth. But in the short time I interviewed him and by the time I'd done the research, I realized that this was a man who had been down a difficult road, who had had his share of prejudice and defeat and difficulty, of troubled economic circumstances. He was also a man who thought about things, who had a philosophy, and that philosophy came out of really thinking through—almost from the beginning—the process of his life. He was somebody who had said, "You don't have to just take what comes along. You can start with a blank sheet of paper, and you take something old and something new and something original and put it all together and interface those pieces to create something." So, I was quite impressed with him, and then once I started seeing his films, I was even more impressed with him because I realized that he was able to translate that art onto the screen.

And today when you look back, how do you think that has maybe changed your life, as far as your once-in-a-lifetime opportunity to talk with him, to do this book, and everything else?

My life has been changed by my contact with Bruce Lee. It's hard to separate the interview I did, from the research I did, from the book that I wrote, to the experiences it has brought me, to the people I've met and been in touch with. This book has touched my life not only then, but also all the way through the years— even in the last couple of years, in part because of the release of the movie about his life story, *Dragon: The Bruce Lee Story*, that was done by Rob Cohen. I got involved in that as well as a documentary that was done about his life, as well as contact with his brother and his sisters, who remain friends of mine, and the brief contacts I've had with Linda Lee, who I think is a lovely lady. I've been inspired by all of these, and I've *learned* from them.

It's really touched my life in many, many different ways. It's odd, because I am someone who grew up in sort of a pacifistic environment. I am more of a writer than a warrior, and yet the contact with Bruce Lee and the physical things that it led me to do, and the associations that it has given me, have kind of given me an entrée into a different world. It's allowed me to see some things I might not have otherwise seen, and to meet people I might not have otherwise met. So, I feel I owe Bruce Lee a debt of gratitude in that sense. I think I did something for him, in that I wrote the first book that accurately reflected his life. And, then, of course, I got to see many, many magazine articles and other books that stole freely from my book without giving it credit. Even a gentleman who wrote for the *Village Voice* said to me, "We stole so much out of your book for our article that we were so embarrassed that we didn't put your name in it at all!"

You, of course, interviewed many people who were friends and students of Bruce Lee's. Was there anyone in particular who struck you as having a really firm grasp of Bruce's philosophy?

There were a number of people that I talked to during that period, particularly some people in Hong Kong, who were quite affecting. I talked to the producers of his films. I talked to some of his students. There was a gentleman in Seattle who had been one of his best friends and also one of his students, Taky Kimura, and he had been profoundly affected by Bruce. His entire life development had been shaped by his contact with Bruce. I think he embodied very much, of all the people I've met then or since, someone who really had understood that Bruce Lee wasn't just some immigrant guy who knew how to fight, but rather was a thoughtful human being with a philosophy that he wanted to share. He also understood that the physical part of it was important; that self-defense and understanding how to use the arts that Bruce taught were also part of it. I think that he represented as much as anyone the ideal of how Bruce influenced people's lives.

In The Legend of Bruce Lee *there is a wonderful passage that explains to westerners what you touched upon earlier about the great traditions, and how the arts were like religion to these people. You describe the inner sanctum of the Shaolin Temple and what these people had to go through simply to get out of the Shaolin Temple. Could you recount some of that?*

The wonderful thing about some of these arts is that, not only do they take it seriously, but also it affects the way that they live their life. A favorite story of mine that I recounted in the book embodies both the difficulty of this art and the magic.

The story goes that a young man who was a student decided that he wanted to become a great warrior. He wanted to learn from the High Priest of one of the great temples. It was during the winter. He knocked on the door of the temple, and they said, "What do you want?" He said, "I want to be a student." And they said to him, "Well, then, stay there on the doorstep, and we'll call you in when we're ready to make you a student." Days went by, and weeks went by, and then several months went by. It was freezing, bitter cold, yet this young man stayed there and he waited, and he waited, and he waited. Finally the door opened, and they said, "OK, you can come in now." And the young man said, "Oh, good. Can I start my instruction?" They said, "No, follow me, and I'll show you what you're going to do."

They led him into the kitchen, and in the kitchen they said, "Here, peel some potatoes and chop up some vegetables, and we'll let you know when you're ready for the next lesson." So he did it, and he did it for a few days and a few weeks and several months. Finally he went to the old master, and he said, "I think you're just using me for free kitchen help! I think this whole thing is a rip-off! You don't know anything, and I'm tired of this! This is all a big, phony deal!" And the master said to him, "It's not a phony deal, and in fact, it's time for your next lesson to begin. Now go back to the kitchen and finish preparing lunch."

So, the young man went back to the kitchen. He was standing there, and then suddenly there was his old bearded master. He had a broad sword in his hands. He was right next to the young man, and he started whacking him with the flat side of this broad sword on the sides of his legs and on his back.

The young man screamed and jumped back. He said, "What are you doing?" The old master said, "You didn't see me coming. When you see me coming, then you will understand the meaning of this lesson." And the old man seemed to disappear again. This went on for days and weeks and months more. The young man never knew where the master was going to come from, whether it was in his bedroom, or in a hallway, or in the kitchen, or anywhere on the grounds. The master would suddenly be there. He seemed to come out of nowhere. And he would whack him with that sword!

Well, finally the young man got to the point where he knew when the master was coming. His senses had become so acute and so finely tuned that he was able to jump back and know when the master came. And when the master could no longer whack him with the sword without being observed first, the master said to him,

"And now it is time for you to learn how to fight yourself." And then he gave him the full instruction.

So, what is the lesson here? The lesson is that you have to pay some dues; that you don't get it easily; that you're going to have to earn it one way or another. But once you get it, you're going to learn something that is going to change your life and be magical in terms of how you can live from then on.

You mentioned "Now it is time for you to learn how to fight yourself": that was something that Bruce himself also touched upon; that the martial artist's techniques were actually directed inward—not outward—and if you are successful, you will be able to "knock out" your ego, or your fears or your hang-ups.

That was a key tenet of Bruce Lee's philosophy, that only when you essentially understand the Zen concept of "nothingness," when you can go back to the point of total "zero," can you become something.

Throughout the course of your interview, what Lee tends to stress is "honest self-expression." How would you interpret that?

The total honesty of his philosophy, not just what he spoke, but his fighting art, was really what he was about. It disturbed him that people would have these elaborate, ritual martial arts movements that would require a great deal of swinging of arms and legs before anything really happened. He said, "What do I need that for? Let's just cut through it."

One of my favorite stories in the book came out of an interview I did in Hong Kong: the story of Bruce Lee being on a talk show. They had all the different masters of the martial arts on this show, and each of them got up and did a demonstration of their different arts. One man got up and said, "I'm going to show you how I can push and punch and do all these different things." He demonstrated, and then he challenged Bruce to get up. He expected Bruce to do some elaborate ritual and all this stuff, and Bruce just got up and cold-cocked him! He knocked him out cold on the stage. And when they said to him, "Why did you do that?" Bruce said, "Because I don't push—I punch."

We talked about how some contemporary martial artists have tried to cash in on Bruce's success. And while some of these individuals' films have grossed more money, because of the higher ticket prices and so on these days, the quality just isn't there. For some reason, as you've touched on, they've missed out on the philosophy of it. They tend to preach it in the dojo, but when they get before the cameras, it's all bravado and macho and "John Wayne with kicks." Is there anyone on the horizon whom you've seen who might be grasping the significance of Bruce or what he taught?

I don't think there's been anyone in the last 25 years who can hold a candle to him in terms of what he did.

And there are some fine human beings who've trained very hard and who've tried very hard to make movies, including some who were friends of Bruce. And then there were those who had a different philosophy. Jackie Chan was really more of a comedic performer who incorporated martial arts into his routine. Chuck Norris has certainly made a lot of interesting action movies and television shows. And there have been many, many others, but nobody has touched Bruce.

Is there anybody coming along? We all know who the current action stars are. Someone like Steven Seagal, perhaps, in his own way as a practitioner of aikido does have a philosophy and to some extent does try to bring it into his films. His most recent film that I saw was about the environment, and the message basically was: "Be kind to the environment, or I'll *kill* you!" In the end, what people remembered were the violence, the action, and the explosions, rather than any philosophy. There just isn't anybody I know of on the scene who is comparable. That doesn't mean they're bad, because each is original in his own way, and there's an audience for what they do. But there's nobody who has that combination of the physical, the mental, and the emotional skills that Bruce was able to bring to the screen.

So, what can people learn from him? What lessons are out there?

I think there are things to be learned from Bruce Lee, and I think it depends on how you want to learn it. If you want to learn by watching his movies, you'd probably get one lesson. If you want to read the writings he left behind, the philosophy, or read the things that people who knew him had to say, you'll get another. And if you do all of that—if you see the movies, read the words, and hear what other people had to say—I think what you learn is that you should not be caught up in the traditions of the past at the expense of learning how to live the future properly.

Bruce Lee was someone who really believed that you took the best of the past. He would never trash something; whether it was a martial art or a great painting, I don't think he would have said, "Throw it all away. Let's have a revolution and start all over again!" Instead, I think he would have said, "Let's take the beautiful building, and the beautiful painting, and the beautiful thought, and let's take the martial arts thought from the Japanese, from the Indonesians, from the Koreans, from the Chinese. Let's take the best of all of it and find out how we can turn that into the world of the future, so we can live better, so we can be better people, so we can get along and coexist in an ever more complex and difficult universe. I think that was Bruce Lee's message, that we can take what was good, but we can also have original thoughts, and we can put it all together so that we can move forward in a way that will allow us to enjoy the fruits of the past but also take advantage of the future.

Perhaps before we close this would be a pertinent question: when you conducted the interview in 1972, when you hung up the phone from speaking with Bruce Lee, what part of the conversation stuck out in your mind the most?

You have to remember that when I hung up the phone, I was totally frustrated that I couldn't make the tape recorder work right and that it had this electronic hum running throughout it, and that he kept saying to me, "I have to go now," and I couldn't ask all the questions that I wanted to ask. What stuck with me was that I had talked to a very smart, very brave, very clear-thinking, philosophical young man who really had a gift, and who really had something to give to the world. He was very impressive. It was very exciting to talk to him, and I only wished it could have been longer and that I would have had more chances to talk to him.

Index

Aikido, 5
Asian Americans, 81–82

Berton, Pierre
  discovery of Lee, 22–23
  impression of Lee on,
    24–26, 30–31
  reasons for Lee's
    popularity, 28
  views on Hong Kong, 29
Big Boss, The, 2, 4, 34,
    37–38, 70–72
Block, Alex Ben, 50
  impression of Lee on,
    87–88
  interview of Lee and,
    78–80
Boxing, 43
  Chinese, 5, 8–9, 66
  shadow, 9–10
  Western, 8–9

Chan, Jackie, 83, 95
China, opening of, 19

Chinese boxing, 5, 8–9,
    66
Chinese dramas, 15
Chinese martial arts. *See*
    Martial arts
Chow, Raymond, 46, 57,
    70, 71
Coburn, James, 3, 7–8,
    10–11, 25, 36, 67
Cohen, Rob, 88

Dialogue, in movies, 4
Dozier, William, 68
Dragon: The Bruce Lee Story,
    88

Eastwood, Clint, 86
Enter the Dragon, 2, 72–73,
    76, 84–85

Fighting. *See* Martial arts
Fighting styles, 42–43
Films. *See* Movies
Fist of Fury, 71–72

Fists of Fury. See Big Boss, The

Franciscus, James, 14, 69

Garner, James, 3, 6, 10
Golden Harvest film company, 57
Green Hornet, The, 11, 17, 40, 68
Gung fu. See Chinese boxing

Hollywood (Calif.), 5
Honesty
    Bruce Lee's philosophy of, 93–94
    martial arts and, 11
Hong Kong, 29, 30
Humor, Bruce Lee and, 86

Imitators, Bruce Lee, 85–86, 94–95

James Dean Syndrome, 28
Jeet kune do, 63–64, 67, 70
Judo, 43

Karate, 5
Kimura, Taky, 90

Korean karate, 5
Kung fu, 24

Lee, Bruce. *See also* individual films of
    acting roles of, 25–26
    as actor, 39–41, 74
    attitudes toward, 81–83
    childhood, 60–61
    death of, 55–56
    dubbing voice of, 53–54
    early acting career, 68–69
    education, 60–61
    effect of, on martial arts films, 29–30
    family, 66
    goal of, in films, 54–55
    hobbies, 67
    Hollywood training schools of, 5
    imitators of, 85–86, 94–95
    on importance of motion, 4
    legacy of, 56–57, 96–97
    as martial artist, 5
    martial arts training, 65

nationality, 62
opening of China, and
   career of, 19
people challenging,
   34–36, 49–50, 74
philosophy of, 14, 24,
   64–65, 84, 93–94
physical measurements,
   62
reaction of Hong Kong
   people to, 30
religion of, 62–63
sense of family and,
   86–87
sense of humor, 86
on speaking Cantonese
   in movies, 3–4
stardom and, 15–16,
   23–24, 40, 41
success of, 74–76
view of self, 20, 26
workouts and, 53
Lee, David, 47
Lee Hoi Chuen, 61
Legend of Bruce Lee, The,
   78
Lo Wei, 70, 71
Longstreet series, 13–14,
   26–27, 69

McQueen, Steve, 3, 6, 10,
   36, 67, 86
Mandarin movies, 3, 4
Martial arts, 66
   defined, 5
   honesty and, 11
   philosophy of, 11
   reasons for learning,
      6–7
   as religion, 80
   styles and, 8
Martial arts films, 29–30
Marvin, Lee, 3, 10
Motion, importance of, in
   movies, 4
Movies
   Mandarin, 3, 4
   martial arts, 29–30

Norris, Chuck, 72, 83, 95

Philosophy
   Bruce Lee on, 4, 14, 24,
      64–65, 84, 93–94
   martial arts and, 11
Polanski, Roman, 10

Religion, Bruce Lee and,
   62–63

Run Run Shaw, 57

Seagal, Steven, 25, 95
Shadow boxing, 9–10
Silliphant, Stirling, 13–14,
    67, 70
Stardom, Bruce Lee on,
    15–16, 23–24
Styles
  fighting, 42–43
  martial arts, 8
Suttcliffe, Charles, 55

Tai chi chuan. *See* Shadow
    boxing
Thomas, Ted, 34
  boxing with Lee and,
      51–52
  discovery of Lee, 46–47

impact of Lee on,
    55–56
impression of Lee,
    48–49
interviews of Lee,
    50–51
relationship with Lee,
    54

Valentino, Rudolph, 57
Van Damme, Jean-Claude,
    25, 83

Western boxing, 8–9
Wilson, Ian, 53
Wing chun, 66

Yip Man, 65
Yu, Wong, 47